Short Sharp Shakespeare Stories

THE Tempest

Retold by Anna Claybourne
Illustrated by Tom Morgan-Jones

WAYLAND
www.waylandbooks.co.uk

First published in 2014 by Wayland

Copyright © Wayland 2014
Wayland
338 Euston Road
London NW1 3BH

Wayland Australia
Level 17/207 Kent Street
Sydney, NSW 2000

Editor: Elizabeth Brent
Design: Amy McSimpson
Illustration: Tom Morgan-Jones

A catalogue for this title is available
from the British Library
Dewey number: 823.9'2-dc23

10 9 8 7 6 5 4 3 2 1

ISBN: 978 0 7502 9115 6
eBook ISBN: 978 0 7502 8811 8
Library eBook ISBN: 978 0 7502 9361 7

Printed in China
Wayland is a division of Hachette Children's Books,
an Hachette UK company
www.hachette.co.uk

WAYLAND
www.waylandbooks.co.uk

SAINT BENEDICT CATHOLIC
VOLUNTARY ACADEMY
DUFFIELD ROAD
DERBY
DE22 1JD

CONTENTS

INTRODUCING *THE TEMPEST*

Shakespeare wrote many plays about kings and queens, romance and friendship, war, murder and revenge. But only one of his works, *The Tempest*, is about a wizard who lives on a magical island. It's one of his last plays, and one of his best-loved comedies.

Who was Shakespeare?

William Shakespeare lived and worked just over 400 years ago in London, England. He was part of a major theatre company, and wrote his plays for them to perform. His shows were so exciting, emotional and powerful that today, they are still popular, and still performed all the time.

What's the story?

Thrown out of his dukedom by his jealous brother Antonio, the wizard Prospero has spent 12 years on a lonely island with his daughter Miranda. Now, Antonio is sailing close by, with King Alonso and his son Ferdinand. Prospero grabs his chance to conjure up a storm (or tempest) and shipwreck them. Can he take his revenge and reclaim power? Read on to begin the stormy, enchanted story of *The Tempest*.

The Tempest: Who's who?

The Tempest begins, like every Shakespeare play,
with a list of characters, called the *dramatis personae*.

MIRANDA

daughter of

Caliban
a monstrous savage
of the island

Ariel
an airy spirit

PROSPERO
a wizard and former
Duke of Milan

brother of

Trinculo
the king's jester*

Stephano
the king's butler

Antonio ⟹ friend of ⟹ Sebastian

brother of

Ship's captain,
boatswain* and sailors
(All Shakespeare
plays feature minor
characters like these.)

Prince Ferdinand

Gonzalo   advisor to

father of

Alonso
King of Naples

* What does that mean!?

A boatswain is a foreman on a ship, who directs the crew.
A jester is a clown or joker who entertains people.

Chapter One

"Boatswain!" the captain bellowed, over the roaring
of the wind and thunder. "Tell the men to take the sails
down! Quick, or we'll be wrecked! There's an island here!"

"Topsail down, jump to it, lads!" the boatswain
ordered. It wasn't the worst storm he'd ever seen
– he could handle this. "Do your
best, wind!" he laughed
into the storm.

"I say!" someone barked in his ear. "Where's the
captain? Is everything all right? It's a bit windy!" The
boatswain turned around and saw King Alonso himself.
He and his royal retinue – his son Ferdinand, his brother
Sebastian, his advisor Gonzalo, and Antonio, Duke of Milan
– had all come up on deck.

"You can't be here, your majesty!"
the boatswain yelled, as politely
as possible. "Sirs, go below, and
shelter in your cabins! Let the
men do their work, or else this
tempest will take us all!"

"Don't forget who you're
speaking to!" warned
Gonzalo. "This is the
king's ship, you know!"

6

"Well if the king would like to command the wind to stop blowing, and the waves to stop rolling," shouted the boatswain, "I'll happily hand over to him. Otherwise, out of our way, please!"

But it was too late. "The ship is lost!" cried the lookout from the top of the mast. "We're heading for the rocks!"

"Abandon ship!" screamed the boatswain. "Jump and swim, my lords – it's your only hope!" And with that, he threw off his jacket and plunged head first into the heaving foam, as the the ship began to keel over.

"Oh please, not drowning, anything but that!" cried poor old Gonzalo as he faced the waves. "What I wouldn't give now for the tiniest patch of dry land!"

A moment later, along with everyone else who had been on board, he was underwater, swimming for his life.

All lost! To prayers, to prayers! All lost! Farewell, brother! Mercy on us!

What does that mean!?
The sailors cry that they are all lost, or doomed, and call on each other to pray,

"Father!" Miranda came running into the little shelter, built around a cave, that had been her home for as long as she could remember.

"Father, did you start this storm, with your magic? You did, didn't you? I've just seen a whole ship wrecked by a storm and smashed to pieces on the rocks. Yet here, it's calm and quiet."

Her father looked up from a large, ancient book. "Don't worry, my dear," he said. "I promise you, there's no harm done."

"No harm!? I heard them screaming! Those poor people, they can't have survived!"

"Miranda, please believe me," Prospero put his book aside, and came over to her.

Oh, the cry did knock against my very heart! Poor souls, they perished!

What does that mean!?
Miranda says the screaming she heard made her heart pound, and she's sure the sailors died (perished).

"I did do this, but only for good reasons. I did it to help you. There are some things that have to be put right, and now is the time to do it."

"To help me?" said Miranda, feeling puzzled. "And what things?"

"Well..." Prospero began, "there's a lot about me that you don't know. It probably seems to you that we've always lived here – and that all I am is your poor old father, with nothing to his name but a little hut and a few magic books."

"I've never really thought about it,"
said Miranda.

"I've never told you anything else,"
said her father. "You were too young
to understand. But now you're 15 –
and I think you are old enough."

"So tell me," Miranda pleaded. "Because I can't see how sending
a ship full of poor, innocent sailors to their deaths can possibly
help anyone."

"Firstly, no one has died," said Prospero. "Everyone on that ship is safe – not one is even hurt. Now sit down and listen. Look at you, Miranda, so grown-up. When we came here you were just a little girl – no more than three years old. Do you remember anything from before that time?"

"I do remember something," Miranda said. "But I always thought it was just a dream I'd had. I remember kind, pretty ladies looking after me, and playing with me. Were they real?"

"Your nannies!" smiled Prospero. "Yes, they were. You were a princess, Miranda, and I was a duke – of the great city of Milan. Your poor mother died when you were a tiny baby. So your nannies looked after you, while I went to work."

"Then what happened?"

"Well, I wasn't a very good duke, I'm afraid," Prospero admitted. "I spent too much time with my nose in my books, and not enough dealing with my duties. So my brother Antonio offered to help me out.

"It turned out he was very good at politics – too good, in fact. He liked the taste of power. He had a friend, Sebastian, who was the brother of King Alonso of Naples. Together, they persuaded Alonso to make Antonio the Duke of Milan, instead of me."

"That's terrible!" gasped Miranda, shocked that anyone could be so mean.

"So, one night, guards came and dragged me from my bed. I picked you up, my beloved little girl, and they hurried us out of the city gates."

"Why didn't they just kill us?" Miranda asked.

"They knew the people of Milan loved me," said Prospero. "If we'd been murdered, they would have suspected Antonio. So the guards put us in a tiny, leaky boat, and pushed us out to sea."

"Why didn't we starve? How did we get here?"

"That was thanks to Gonzalo, a good, kind advisor to the King," said Prospero. "He had hidden food and water in the boat – as well as clothes and other useful things. He even packed my magic books. And so we survived, until we came to this island."

"I wish I could meet Gonzalo, and thank him," said Miranda.

"Well, my dear, that brings me to today," Prospero went on. "By chance, Antonio, Sebastian and the King were sailing past the island, on their way home from a wedding. Using my magic, I conjured up a tempest to cast their ship ashore. Now they are trapped here, and I have some important business with them. But that's enough for now," Prospero said, seeing Miranda yawn. "You're exhausted."

Miranda lay down on her bed, and was asleep in seconds.

Oh, a cherubim Thou wast that didst preserve me. Thou didst smile, Infused with a fortitude from heaven.

What does that mean!?
Prospero tells Miranda that having her with him saved his live or "preserved" him, giving him strength, or "fortitude".

"Now, Ariel, come," called Prospero. In the air above him appeared a strange spirit – a translucent, flying, shape-shifting creature. He took on a more human form, like a fairy, and danced in front of Prospero. "What do you wish, my master?"

"Did you do as I asked, my spirit?"

"Yes, my master! All the terror of thunder and lightning, the wind raging and the waves roaring, I cast upon the ship, and into the sea they all leapt!"

"But are they safe?"

"Indeed, my master, I rescued every one. None is harmed –   they're fresher and cleaner than before! I've left them all ashore around the island. The ship I mended too, and there she bobs in the bay, the crew all sound asleep."
"You've done well, my clever spirit," said Prospero.

"So you will give me my freedom, sir?"

"Soon," said Prospero. "When I came here, Ariel, I freed you from the tree where the witch Sycorax had left you, trapped inside the trunk. In return, you have served me well. I have only a few more jobs for you. After that, you will be free."

Miranda was stirring, so Prospero quickly whispered his instructions to Ariel, who flew off.

"Come on, Miranda," Prospero called. "It's time to visit Caliban."

Caliban was as different from Ariel as it was possible for a creature to be. He was a great, hulking, hairy, snaggle-toothed beast, half-man, half monster. He too was Prospero's servant.

"Come out of your cave, Caliban, you lazy layabout!" Prospero called.

"May poisonous winds blow on you," Caliban grumbled as he emerged. "What do you want?"

"We need firewood for this evening," said Prospero.

"I was just about to have my dinner," Caliban complained. "You've got enough firewood. And anyway it's not your wood. This is my island – it belonged to my mother, Sycorax the witch, and now she's dead, it's mine."

"Caliban, you know I tried to be kind to you, and let you live in my own home," said Prospero wearily. "And how did you repay me? You attacked my innocent daughter. You can't be trusted, and that's why I keep you here, in your own cave, and use magic to control you."

"A plague of toads and beetles on you!" Caliban cursed, but he obeyed Prospero, and headed off to collect firewood from the forest.

As he went, a young man came wandering out of the woods. It was Ferdinand, King Alonso's son. Ahead of him flew Ariel, playing on a harp. But the prince couldn't see him, and had no idea where the sound was coming from.

Now, as he strummed the strings, Ariel began to sing a strange, sad song.

What does that mean!?

Ariel's song says that Alonso lies five fathoms deep in the sea, and instead of rotting, his body has been turned into coral and pearls.

> Full fathom five thy father lies,
> Of his bones are coral made,
> Those are pearls that were his eyes.
> Nothing of him that doth fade,
> But doth suffer a sea-change
> Into something rich and strange.

"My father?" gasped Ferdinand. "Who's singing? Is my father the King drowned?"

Miranda's eyes almost popped out of her head. This was the first man she had seen, apart from Prospero and Caliban, for 12 years. And he was far more handsome than either of them!

"Who is THAT!?" she exclaimed.

"He's just a human, like you, my dear," said Prospero.
"A survivor from the ship."

Ferdinand saw Miranda, and gazed at her in awe. "Beautiful maiden," he gasped. "Was that you I heard singing? If I could, I'd marry you, and make you queen of Naples. For I fear my father has been lost in a shipwreck, and I will have to take his place as king."

Miranda blushed, and Prospero smiled to himself – things were turning out just as he planned. But he couldn't let Ferdinand win his daughter's love so easily. "Well, young man," he interrupted. "I've no idea who you are, so until you can prove your worth, you can come and do some work for me. Firewood needs carrying. This way!"

Chapter Two

Though Ferdinand thought his father was dead, of course he wasn't at all. At that moment, King Alonso was sitting sadly on the seashore in another part of the island.

Gonzalo was there too – and Alonso's brother Sebastian, and Antonio, the Duke of Milan. But Ferdinand was nowhere to be seen.

Gonzalo was trying to cheer everyone up. "What a miracle we've all survived!" he exclaimed. "And this island looks alright, doesn't it? I'm sure we can survive here, until someone rescues us."

"Yes, what a delightful barren rock in the middle of nowhere," mocked Sebastian. "Aren't we lucky, being shipwrecked!"

'Twas a sweet wedding, and we prosper well in our return.

What does that mean!? Sebastian sarcastically says the journey back from the wedding has gone brilliantly. "Prosper well" means have good luck.

Antonio joined in with the sneering. "It might be even nicer if there was actually anything to eat, or some fresh water. Then it would be perfect!"

Gonzalo ignored them. "I've noticed something very strange, too. Our clothes are all clean and dry, even though we've just been in the sea! We look as smart as we did at the King's daughter's wedding! I think this island might be enchanted."

"Oh great. We're all going to starve to death, but at least we're nice and smart," said Sebastian.

"Stop it, all of you!" King Alonso groaned. "I wish I'd never let Claribel marry the King of Tunis! Then we wouldn't have had to make this journey, and we wouldn't be shipwrecked, and I wouldn't have lost my son! Oh, Ferdinand! I'm sure he's drowned! Oh my boy, what strange sea creatures are nibbling on you now?"

"Yes, well, we did tell you it wasn't such a great plan, but you insisted," said Sebastian. "It's your own fault."

O thou mine heir... what strange fish Hath made his meal on thee?

"That's not helping, Sebastian!" Gonzalo scolded. "Your Majesty, Ferdinand is an excellent swimmer. I'm sure he's made his way to safety, and we'll find him soon."

Just then, Ariel arrived, invisible, above their heads. Following Prospero's instructions, he played a magical song on his harp, which made Alonso and Gonzalo very sleepy.

"Well, after all that swimming, I feel like a nap!" Gonzalo yawned. A moment later, he and Alonso were snoring on the soft, warm sandy beach.

What does that mean!?
Alonso cries out to Ferdinand, his heir, or son, wondering what fish have eaten him.

"That's weird," Antonio said. "I don't feel sleepy. Do you, Sebastian?"

"No – but I thought I heard a funny sound." They looked all around them, but couldn't see anything.

"Well," said Antonio, "It does seem a bit random that those two are asleep, and we aren't." He looked his friend in the eye. "Almost too good to be true, in fact."

Sebastian stared at him. "You don't mean..."

"Come on, Sebastian. Ferdinand's obviously dead. Claribel's gone off to be the Queen of Tunis. So who's next in line to the throne? You are. All we need to do is get rid of these two, and throw their bodies in the sea. Then, with a bit of luck, we'll be rescued – and between us, we'll rule the whole of Italy."

Sebastian smiled. "For this, my friend, I'll reward you well – once I'm on the throne."

He reached for his dagger, and Antonio took his out too.

"I'll deal with Alonso," Antonio said – it would be a bit much to ask Sebastian to stab his own brother. "You take Gonzalo. He's such an old woman, he'll be no trouble."

Little did they know that Ariel was still watching every move, and listening to every word. As the would-be murderers sneaked towards their victims, Ariel quickly darted down and whispered in Gonzalo's ear: "Wake up!"

"What!? Who's there?" Gonzalo started awake. This woke Alonso too, and he sat up, blinking. "Why have you drawn your daggers?" he asked. "What happened?"

"Erm..." Antonio began. "It was just..."

"The lions!" Sebastian said suddenly. "We heard a terrible noise, like a lion roaring, and we took out our daggers to protect you."

"That's right," Antonio butted in. "It sounded like a whole PACK of lions! Didn't you hear it?"

"There must be wild beasts on this island," said Gonzalo. "Perhaps it's not so safe here after all."

"Let's go and find somewhere else to shelter," said Alonso. "And we can search for Ferdinand, too."

When they had gone, Ariel flew back to Prospero, to tell him everything he had seen.

In the forest, Caliban was trudging to and fro picking up firewood. As he went, he muttered all the meanest curses he could think of.

"I hope Prospero gets sucked into a smelly swamp," he grouched. "I hope he gets so many diseases, he turns INTO a disease."

Just then, he heard a sound in the forest, "Oh, no," he groaned. "Here comes Ariel, checking up on me. Well, I'm not talking to him. I'll lie down here and hide until he goes away." Caliban quickly lay down in a ditch, covered himself up with his cloak, and soon began to snooze.

But the sound he had heard wasn't Ariel. It was Trinculo, King Alonso's jester. He had stayed below the deck when the storm struck, and swum ashore by himself. He had no idea if anyone else had survived the wreck at all – so he was wandering around the island to see who he could find. But clouds were gathering overhead, and it was starting to rain.

"Just my luck," sighed Trinculo. "If only I could find some shelter." Then he spotted the huge mound of Caliban's cloak on the ground. He lifted a corner and peered underneath.

"Ewww!" he exclaimed. "What's this? Whatever it is, it's not human! It has legs like a man, but a hairy face like a monster – and it stinks of fish!"

A loud thunderclap shook the forest, and the rain began to pour down on Trinculo's head.

"Well, fish-monster," said Trinculo, "beggars can't be choosers, and I need to shelter from the rain. Budge up." Holding his nose, he climbed under the cloak and lay down next to the snoring Caliban.

As Trinculo had wrapped some of the cloak around himself, Caliban's head was now sticking out, and Stephano almost tripped over it.

Stephano was the King's butler, and Trinculo's friend. He had floated ashore on a wooden crate, and when he opened it, he found it was full of wine. He was carrying several bottles with him as he stumbled through the forest, and he had already started drinking one of them.

29

"Aaaarrrrgh!" Stephano screamed, as Caliban opened one eye. "What on Earth is that!? A huge, hairy monster!" He spotted the two pairs of legs sticking out from the other end of the cloak. "A huge, hairy monster with four legs!" he wailed.

Caliban thought Prospero had sent a spirit to punish him for falling asleep. "Don't hurt me!" he whimpered.

"You poor monster, I won't hurt you," said Stephano. "Here, have some wine." He put the open bottle to Caliban's mouth.

Under the cloak, Trinculo heard a voice he knew well. "Stephano?" he called.

"Aaarrggh – a huge, hairy monster with four legs and two mouths!" cried Stephano.

"You idiot, it's me, Trinculo!" shouted Trinculo, emerging from the cloak. The rain had stopped, and he stood up. "Stephano, you're alive! I was just sharing this fish-monster's cloak."

Meanwhile, Caliban was guzzling from the bottle. It was the most amazing drink he'd ever tasted.

"What a wondrous, kind master," Caliban said to Stephano. "In return for the drink you have given me, I'll show you where to find food – where to go fishing, and find the best

berries and nuts, and the sweetest spring water.
I'll be your servant."

"That sounds OK to me!" said Stephano.

"Lead on, monster!" Trinculo
laughed. And they all headed
off through the forest,
slurping wine and
singing sea shanties.

Chapter Three

Outside Prospero's hut, Ferdinand was hard at work stacking logs into a pile, as Prospero had instructed him.

"You poor thing – sit down and have a rest!" Miranda begged him. "My father's reading inside, so he won't see you. I could carry a few logs while you have a break."

"My lady, I couldn't let you do that!" Ferdinand protested. "This may be hard work, but I do it with a happy heart – because I'm doing it for you. I only want to please your father, so I can ask him if he'll let me marry you." Miranda blushed bright pink.

"I've loved you from the moment I saw you," Ferdinand said, "but I don't even know your name. Please tell me it."

"My father told me not to – but I will. It's Miranda."

"Miranda," Ferdinand repeated. "Do you know what 'Miranda' means?"

"No... Oh sir, I'm afraid I don't know much about the world at all."

"It means 'admired' – and that's perfect, because I admire you more than I can say. You're lovelier than any woman I've ever met."

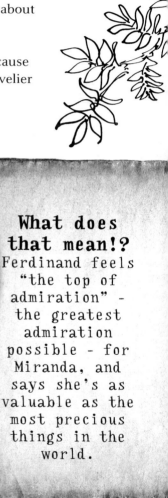

Admired Miranda! Indeed the top of admiration! Worth what's dearest to the world.

What does that mean!? Ferdinand feels "the top of admiration" - the greatest admiration possible - for Miranda, and says she's as valuable as the most precious things in the world.

"I haven't met many other men," Miranda replied. "But I know you're the only one I want. I'd gladly be your wife." They gazed into each other's eyes.

Inside the hut, Prospero was not reading. He was watching quietly through the window.

"Excellent," he smiled. "I may never feel the joy of young love again, like those two, but still, I couldn't be happier."

His plan was going perfectly. But there was a lot to do before the end of the day, and he would need his most powerful magic.

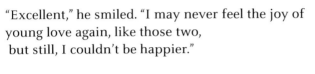

By now, Caliban, Stephano and Trinculo had reached Caliban's cave, and had drunk a lot more of the wine. Before long, they began to argue.

"You're my master," Caliban told Stephano. "I'll do anything you ask. But I won't obey this idiot here."

"Well that's nice!" Trinculo complained. "Who do you think you are, fish-face!?"

"He's teasing me, my lord – tell him to stop!" Caliban whined to Stephano.

"Ha! That's a good one," said Trinculo.

"That's the first time I've heard a butler being called a lord!"

"Silence on my island!" Stephano smirked. "You heard the monster. I'm the boss now."

"You can be king of the island," Caliban said, "but you will have to kill Prospero – the evil magician who stole it from me, and made me his slave."

"You're lying" sang a voice behind them. It was Ariel, but Caliban thought it was Trinculo. "I'm not lying!" he cried. "Master, he's teasing me again!"

"Shut up, Trinculo," Stephano said. "OK, if the island is run by an evil wizard, how do I kill him?"

Caliban sidled closer, and whispered: "Every afternoon, Prospero has a nap. I'll take you to his hut, and you can stab him. Or bash his brains in with a log. Whatever you like. It'll be easy."

"You lie," called Ariel again.

"Right, Trinculo, you're annoying me now," said Stephano, and gave him a shove.

"I didn't say anything!" Trinculo shouted, pushing him back.

"And then," Caliban went on, "you'll be king, and you can marry the wizard's beautiful daughter."

Stephano turned back to the monster. "He has a beautiful daughter, too? Right, that's convinced me. Let's do it. I'll be the king, she'll be the queen – and you two can be our trusted royal advisors. OK?"

"Oh, alright," said Trinculo. "Let's go and find this wizard."

But before they could set off, Ariel took out a flute again, and played a mysterious, enchanting tune.

Be not afeard; the isle is full of noises, Sounds and sweet airs, that give delight and hurt not.

"What's that!?" said Stephano.

"Oh, don't fear the sounds of the island," said Caliban. "That's always happening."

"It's beautiful," said Trinculo. "Let's follow it, just for a little while. We can find that wizard later." And they stumbled off in the wrong direction.

Meanwhile, the King, Antonio, Sebastian and Gonzalo were trudging through the trees in their search for Ferdinand.

"This is like wandering around inside a maze!" said Gonzalo. "I need a rest." He sat down on a rock.

"I don't blame you, old man," said the King, sitting next to him. "This is hopeless. Ferdinand's gone. He's out there, under the waves. I know it." He wiped away a tear.

"They're getting tired again," Antonio said to Sebastian, under his breath. "Have your dagger ready – we'll get another chance soon."

"Next time they drop off, we'll do it," Sebastian agreed.

"What's that sound?" said Gonzalo. "Listen."

What does that mean!?
"Afeard" means afraid, and
"airs" means tunes. Caliban
says the island is full
of sounds, but they are
harmless.

Soft, sweet music was filling the air in the forest. In front of their
eyes, the four men saw strange, transparent figures – fairies, or
ghosts – stepping through the trees. They carried dishes of food,
which they put down carefully in a clearing.

The music became quieter, and the figures vanished – but the food was still there. It looked delicious – plates of pies and pastries, cakes, fruit and cheese.

"It is a magic island!" said Gonzalo.

"Now I'll believe anything!" said Antonio. "We all know sailors tell tall tales about enchanted islands. Maybe they're true after all!"

"Let's try some of this food," said Sebastian.

"Not me," said King Alonso. "What if it's a trick? It could be poisoned."

"Don't worry, your Majesty," said Gonzalo. "It's good magic, I'm sure of it. And we're so hungry."

"You're right," Alonso sighed. "Who cares if it's my last meal, anyway? I'll never see my son again, so I'm past caring." With that, he stepped forward and reached for a slice of pie.

CRASH! There was a noise like thunder, and the sky turned dark. Alonso cowered in horror as a huge, winged demon with glowing red eyes – Ariel, in one of his many disguises – appeared above the banquet. It flapped its wings, and the food vanished. Then the terrifying creature spoke.

CRASH!

You **three**
From Milan did supplant
good Prospero.

What does that mean!?
Ariel reminds the men
that they "supplanted", or
replaced, Prospero as duke
of Milan, and threw him out. 41

"Three evil men I see," it boomed. "So repulsive, even the sea could not bring itself to swallow you – so it vomited you up onto our shore."

Alonso and Sebastian drew their daggers, but the demon laughed. "Your knives can't hurt me," it sneered, "and they can't hurt Prospero.

"Yes, Prospero," the creature roared, as Alonso hid his face in shame. "I know what you three did. You betrayed him, and cast him out, him and his little child, into the sea. And now the sea has punished you. It's risen up against your ship, King Alonso, and taken away your son. And it serves you right."

CRASH! With another thunderclap, the demon disappeared, and the sun shone again.

"Your Majesty? What's the matter?" asked Gonzalo. He hadn't seen a thing.

"Where's that beast gone!?" said Antonio. "We'll find it and kill it!"

"What beast, my lords?" Gonzalo asked.

"D-didn't you see it?" Alonso gibbered. "That monster, that great big terrible thing? It knew, oh Gonzalo, it knew what we did to Prospero, and that's why Ferdinand has drowned – to punish me! Oh my boy, I'm sorry! Let me come and join you, and we'll lie there together!"

But before Alonso could run into the sea, Ariel cast another spell on the men. It sent them all into a trance, and not one of them could move a muscle.

Chapter Four

Ferdinand had been carrying logs for three whole hours. His face was wet with sweat and his hands were full of splinters, and Prospero was sorry he had tested him so harshly. He came out of his hut.

"Stop, Prince Ferdinand, stop and rest," he said. The test is over. I'm sorry I made you work so hard, but I had to see if you were worthy of my daughter. You've proved yourself – and I give my consent for you to marry her. If she'll have you, that is."

"Of course I will!" Miranda jumped up and ran to Ferdinand, and they hugged and kissed.

"Then it's all arranged," said Prospero. "Soon, we will leave this island, and back in Italy, the wedding will take place. Now, come and sit down together, you two. I have something to show you."

He called Ariel to his side, and whispered to him. The spirit darted away and soon returned with a troop of fairies. One was dressed as Juno, goddess of the sky, and another as Ceres, goddess of the soil, crops and harvests. A third was Iris, the rainbow that joins them together.

As the fairies danced, they sang:

Let Ceres leave her fields of peas and corn
To meet with Juno, goddess of the sky.
The caring sky sends showers and dewdrops down
To feed the fields and make the crops grow high.

Husbands and wives are like the sky and Earth.
Together they make children grow up tall.
Wrapped in a rainbow, let us bless you both,
And make your marriage happiest of all.

Ferdinand and Miranda laughed as the colourful fairies danced and weaved in and out around them.

But Prospero was looking worried. He had just remembered something. "Caliban's plot," he said, frowning. "I must stop him, and those silly servants he's ganged up with. They could ruin everything."

As the fairy dancers faded away into the air, Prospero turned to Ferdinand and Miranda.

"The show is over," he said, a little sadly. "It's ended, just as everything must end. Our life here on this island, indeed our lives themselves, must end. The towers and palaces, the great cities, probably the whole world – they'll all come to an end one day. They'll dissolve and disappear, and seem like nothing more than a dream."

They stared at him in confusion. "Forgive me, my dears," Prospero said. "I'm just an old man blathering on. Now, you two stay in the hut. I have a few things to sort out, but I'll be back soon."

The cloud-capp'd **towers**, the gorgeous palaces, The solemn temples, the great globe itself, Yea, all which it inherit, shall dissolve...

What does that mean!?
"Yea" means yes, and "all which it inherit" means everyone who will ever live on Earth.

Following Prospero's instructions, Ariel led Caliban, Stephano and Trinculo through the thickest part of the forest, until they were covered in thorns and nettle-stings. Finally, he lured them into a slimy pond full of frogspawn.

"Shhh," said Caliban. "This pond is close to Prospero's hut. We're nearly there."

"But my boot's stuck, and I smell like a pile of horse dung," Stephano complained.

"And even worse, we've dropped our wine bottles in the mud!" Trinculo moaned.

"Come on," Caliban whispered. "Just follow me, and soon you'll be king of the island, remember?"

Finally Stephano clambered out of the pond, but left his boots behind. Trinculo crawled after him.

49

But Ariel was watching, and as they approached Prospero's
hut, he flew ahead. He tied washing lines between the trees,
then strung them with expensive clothes – suits of the finest
silk, gold-trimmed cloaks, new leather boots and woollen
stockings, and even a glittering crown.

"Look at that, Stephano!"
Trinculo shouted. "Look
– everything you
need to be a king!"

"I certainly need
these boots,"
said Stephano.
"Wow, they fit
perfectly! And I
think this cloak
must be for me
– and the crown,
of course."

"Does this jacket fit me?" Trinculo preened, turning around. "Does it look OK from the back?"

"Come on," Caliban pleaded, "We can come back later. Prospero will get away!"

But they were too late. Ariel called on Prospero, and using his magic, he summoned up a pack of hunting dogs. They snarled and slavered, ripped at the clothes, and chased the three plotters away, to the island's farthest shore.

Chapter Five

Thank you, my spirit," Prospero said. "Our work is almost done, and you will be free very soon. Where are King Alonso and his friends?"

"I followed your orders, sir," Ariel sang. "They are trapped in a trance in the forest, and cannot move. Tears roll down the King's face, in his grief for his son. If you saw it, sir, you would feel sorry."

"Maybe it's time to forgive them," Prospero agreed. "Fetch them, Ariel, and bring them to my hut."

Outside his dwelling, Prospero used a stick to draw a large circle on the ground. "Well, I've had a busy day," he said to himself, as he waited. "I've drummed up a sea storm, smashed a ship to bits, and seen it mended. I've turned the sky dark, then switched the sun back on. I've led my enemies a merry dance, and made fairies dance for my daughter. Magic is a powerful tool, and no mistake.

"But everything comes to an end, and the time has come for me to say goodbye to magic. Once this day is over, I'll throw my books into the sea, where they'll sink so deep, they'll never be seen again."

And deeper than did ever plummet sound, I'll drown my book.

What does that mean!?

Prospero will throw his books into the sea to sink deeper than any depth ever measured by a plummet - a weight lowered into the sea.

53

He looked up to see Ariel leading
King Alonso, followed by Gonzalo,
Sebastian and Antonio, into the
circle. With a snap of his fingers, he
awoke them from their trance.

"Where are we?" Alonso said. His
eyes widened in shock as he realised
who was standing in front of him.
"Prospero?" he gulped. "You're alive?"

"Very much so," Prospero smiled, and
Gonzalo began to weep with joy.
Prospero went and hugged him.

"Gonzalo, my old friend. You saved my life, and Miranda's, 12 years ago, and don't think I've ever forgotten it. Thank you."

"Prospero – I'm so sorry for what I did," King Alonso began. "I listened to evil words, and I let terrible things happen to you. And I've lost my beloved son as a punishment. The dukedom of Milan is yours, Prospero – you can have it back, and I beg you to forgive me."

"I forgive you Alonso," Prospero said, "and I know just how you feel. I've lost my daughter, too."

"Oh, no!" said Alonso. "Your little Miranda! I'm so sorry."

"Yes – just look inside my hut, and you'll see what I mean."
Prospero freed Alonso from the circle, and he opened the door
of the hut. Miranda and Ferdinand were inside, playing a game
of chess.

"My boy!" Alonso cried, and rushed to hug him. "You're alive!"

"And so is my daughter." Prospero said. "But they're leaving us, Alonso, I'm afraid. They're going to get married. I've repaired your ship, your Majesty, and the crew are all safe – and your jester, and your butler too. We'll all sail back to Italy tomorrow, and there we'll have a wedding."

But there were still two people
Prospero had not dealt with.
He went up to Sebastian
and Antonio, and spoke
to them quietly, so
that no one else
could hear.

"I know what you were planning today – to kill Gonzalo, and the king himself." he said. "Here's my offer. I'll forgive you everything, and never breathe a word. But in return you will never do another evil deed as long as you live. Agreed?" The two men nodded sullenly

"Very well," said Prospero. "Ariel, my spirit, come." Ariel flew to him. "My airy spirit, now I set you free," he said. "I'll miss you." Ariel flew up, up and away into the sunset.

Prospero turned back to the others. "Night is falling," he said. "Come inside, and I'll tell you the whole story of how we came here, and our years on this enchanted island. Then, when the dawn breaks, we'll all go home."

THE TEMPEST AT A GLANCE

In Shakespeare's time, comedies weren't meant to be constantly funny, though there are some funny bits. Instead, a comedy meant a play with a love story and a happy ending. Those Shakespeare wrote later in his life, including *The Tempest* and *The Winter's Tale*, are known as the "romances". They tend to have older main characters and a more melancholy atmosphere than his earlier comedies.

The Tempest as a play

In this book, *The Tempest* is retold in prose, but Shakespeare wrote it as a play. This meant it was mainly just lines of speech, or dialogue, along with a few stage directions (instructions for the actors). Here you can see the opening of *The Tempest*, as Shakespeare wrote it. The stage directions explain the setting and sound effects, and who is on stage.

ACT 1

Scene i. ⟦On a ship at sea⟧
A tempestuous noise of thunder and lightning heard.

Enter a Ship-Master and a Boatswain. ⟵ Stage directions

MASTER: Boatswain!
BOATSWAIN: Here, master: what cheer?
MASTER: Good, speak to the mariners: fall to it, yarely, or we run ourselves aground: bestir, bestir!

FACT FILE:
FULL TITLE: *The Tempest*
DATE WRITTEN: around 1610-11
LENGTH: 2,086 lines

Acts and scenes

The Tempest, like Shakespeare's other plays, has five main sections, or acts, divided into smaller sections or scenes. Each scene is set in a different place. Breaking the play into sections allowed playwrights to build a clear structure of events, as well as helping the actors to learn their parts.

THE FIVE ACTS OF *THE TEMPEST*

ACT 1 (2 scenes)

After Prospero creates a storm to shipwreck his enemies on his island, they are all cast ashore in different places.

ACT 2 (2 scenes)

While the King and his friends search for his son Ferdinand, Ferdinand falls in love with Prospero's daughter Miranda.

ACT 3 (3 scenes)

The spirit Ariel makes the King regret throwing Prospero out of his dukedom, and deflects Caliban's plot to kill Prospero.

ACT 4 (1 scene)

Prospero agrees to Ferdinand marrying Miranda.

ACT 5 (1 scene)

Prospero finally confronts everyone, forgives them, gives up his magic, and claims his dukedom back.

THE STORY OF *THE TEMPEST*

Though Shakespeare wrote beautiful and powerful plays, and is famed for his poetic skills, he didn't actually make up his own stories. Usually, he borrowed them from old folktales or legends, or from the history books.

Tale of a shipwreck

For *The Tempest*, Shakespeare turned to an unusual source: a recent news story. The island and the storm are thought to be based on survivors' reports of a real-life shipwreck in 1609. Shakespeare combined this with a type of Italian theatre called the Commedia dell'Arte. It's similar to a pantomime, with traditional characters who include a wizard, his daughter, and a selection of comedy servants.

All in a day

The Tempest is one of the shortest plays Shakespeare wrote. The action all happens in one day and in one place, another theatre tradition, dating from ancient Greece. Some playwrights liked to follow this tradition closely. Shakespeare himself usually ignored it, except for in this play.

One day, one place, one wizard. Simple!

Intertwining plots

The play sets up three groups of characters – the King and his friends, Stephano and Trinculo, and Ferdinand and Miranda – who all find themselves in different parts of the island. It then weaves together their adventures from the time of the shipwreck up until nightfall, when the play ends.

Where was the island?

The island in the play does not have a name, and it's not thought to be a real place. The shipwreck that inspired Shakespeare happened in Bermuda, far out in the Atlantic Ocean. But in the play, the king's ship is returning from Tunis, in north Africa, to Naples, Italy – meaning the island would have to be somewhere in the Mediterranean Sea.

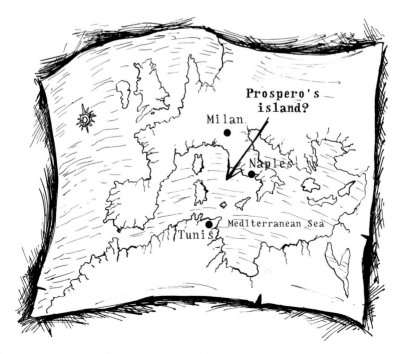

SHAKESPEARE AND *THE TEMPEST*

Why did Shakespeare write *The Tempest*?
As well as being an unusual play in many
ways, it is one of his most personal.

A long career

In the early 1590s, Shakespeare came to London to make a
living as an actor and playwright. In 1594, he joined a new
theatre company, The Chamberlain's Men, who became the
King's Men in 1603 (when the reign of King James began).

Over 16 years, Shakespeare built up a brilliant
career. He became the company's star writer,
famous for his wide-ranging, endlessly
entertaining plays. So, when he
wrote *The Tempest* in around
1610, Shakespeare was partly
doing what he always did –
trying to create a great show
that audiences would enjoy.

That Shakespeare's got a new play out!

Ooh, I love his stuff!

It's goodbye from me!

However, the play can also be seen as a farewell message from Shakespeare. Around this time, he retired and went back to live in his home town, Stratford-upon-Avon, with his family. Many people think the wizard Prospero stands for Shakespeare himself, while the magic represents his creative skills, which he's about to leave behind.

"And to my state grew stranger, being transported and rapt * in secret studies."   *absorbed

In Act 1, Prospero tells Miranda he neglected Milan and ended up in a faraway place, thanks to his books – just as Shakespeare himself left Stratford for London.

In Act 5 Prospero recalls how he has used his magic to conjure up anything he likes – just as a playwright does with words. Then he says:

"But this rough magic I here abjure * "   *give up

Prospero swears he really is finished with his magic, and there's no going back.

"Deeper than did ever plummet sound I'll drown my book"

When Prospero talks about how everything must come to an end, he mentions towers, palaces, temples and "the great globe itself". As well as planet Earth, this also means London's famous Globe Theatre, where the play was almost certainly performed.

STAGING *THE TEMPEST*

The Tempest is very exciting to see on the stage, with its magic spells and visions, spirits, monsters, and the violent sea storm itself. This was true in Shakespeare's time too. There was no film or TV, so people went to the theatre to be entertained and amazed, and theatre companies made a big effort to have the best special effects.

Making magic

How did Shakespeare's company bring *The Tempest* to life?

Flying

Characters like Ariel could "fly" suspended on ropes from the ceiling. The Globe had a roof over the stage with a trapdoor in it, so actors could be lowered out of the "sky".

Appearing from nowhere

There were also trapdoors in the stage, and a large space underneath it. When Ariel appears as a terrifying demon, for example, he could pop up through a trapdoor.

Don't drop me!

Vanishing objects

When the delicious-looking banquet suddenly disappears, Shakespeare includes a stage direction: "With a quaint * device, the banquet vanishes."

✳ "Quaint" meant clever or ingenious

Thunder and lightning

For the loud booming and rumbling sounds of a storm, assistants set off fireworks behind the stage, and rolled heavy cannonballs up and down on the floorboards.

Shakespeare's theatres

By 1610, Shakespeare's theatre company had two main theatres of their own – the open-air Globe Theatre, and the indoor Blackfriars Theatre. Indoor theatres were warmer and could be lit by candles, so they were used for evening and winter performances. *The Tempest* was probably performed in both places.

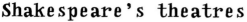

The Globe Theatre was a ring-shaped building with the open-air stage in the middle.

This picture shows what the Blackfriars Theatre may have looked like inside.

67

THE TEMPEST
THEMES AND SYMBOLS

In many of his plays, Shakespeare uses repeated themes and symbols all the way through. They help to hold the play together, give it its own unique atmosphere, and emphasise particular ideas or messages. In *The Tempest* they include:

Magic

The key theme of *The Tempest* is Prospero's magical skill, which acts as a symbol for the playwright's art. Prospero controls everyone on the island, moving them here and there like puppets on strings – just as a playwright does with his or her characters.

But although magic is thrilling and spectacular, Prospero knows it is not true power.
He must leave it behind to return to his real-life responsibilities – his dukedom at home in Milan.

The power of the sea

The sea plays a huge part in *The Tempest*. It surrounds the characters, swallows them up, spits them out, and constantly calls to them. The characters talk about the sea, and who might be drowned in it, throughout the play. It forms the barrier between the magical world of the island, where the action happens, and the real world that is waiting for everyone back home.

It is endlessly deep, wide and powerful, contrasting with the tiny island, and the weakness, smallness and short lifespans of human beings.

Human nature

Caliban and Ariel are real characters – a half-human beast and an airy spirit – but they can also be seen as symbols of the two sides of human nature. They represent two aspects of life on the island for Prospero and his daughter: physical life, having to find food and shelter to survive; and the life of the mind – ideas, thoughts, creativity, memories and plans.

CALIBAN:
Body and physical needs
Caliban eats, sleeps, feels pain and lives in a cave.

ARIEL:
Mind, spirit or soul
Ariel flies, dances, sings, changes shape, and casts spells.

THE MEANING OF MAGIC

When we watch *The Tempest*, we see the magic as a fantastical, imaginary thing – just like the magic in *Harry Potter* or *The Hobbit*. In Shakespeare's time, though, many people really believed magic could happen. It could be used for good or bad, but it was a mysterious, frightening force.

Witches, fairies and gold

In the 1600s, people – especially old women – could be executed if they were suspected of being witches. They were said to fly, talk to animals and cast spells to change the weather or cause diseases. It was also normal to believe in fairies, demons, and magical creatures like mermaids and unicorns.

Another form of magic was alchemy. Alchemists tried to mix different substances in the hope of creating gold, or a potion that would give you everlasting life.

The end of magic

In *The Tempest*, magic is brought under control.
The characters reveal that an evil witch, Sycorax,
once ruled the island – she was Caliban's mother, and used
a spell to trap Ariel inside a tree. But when Prospero arrives,
he replaces her, and undoes her work. He uses his magic
powers to control violence and danger, to make people
pay for their crimes, and finally to return everyone to their
rightful places. Then, at last, he throws his magic books away.

The age of science

This may reflect some of the huge changes that happened
around 1600, the start of a great age of scientific discovery.
Things that had once been explained by supernatural beliefs
– such as stars and planets, electricity, and tales of strange
creatures from far-off lands – were starting to be properly
understood. Alchemy was slowly changing from a magic art
into the modern science of chemistry, as people learned how
substances really changed and interacted.

Around 1600, William Gilbert studied the strange
effects of static electricity and magnetism
in a scientific way.

In 1610, Galileo used the newly
invented telescope to study space,
and see how moons move
around planets.

Explorers were sailing
around the globe,
learning about other
peoples and lands.

THE LANGUAGE OF
THE TEMPEST

Shakespeare wrote his plays mostly in a form of poetry, called blank verse. There were five "beats" or stresses in each line. The lines sometimes rhymed, or contained poetic patterns of words, sounds and images to make them more beautiful and evocative. Different characters had their own language styles, to express their personalities. These speeches from two different parts of the play contain several examples of Shakespeare's poetic style:

Caliban: Be not afeard; the isle is full of noises,*

Sounds and sweet** airs, that give delight and hurt not.

Sometimes a thousand twangling instruments

Will hum about mine ears, and sometime*** voices.*

Prospero: .....they hurried us aboard a bark** (bark means ship)

Bore** us some leagues* to sea*, where they prepared

A rotten carcass of a butt*, not*** rigg'd,

(butt means tub/tiny boat)

Nor*** tackle, sail, nor*** mast; the very rats

Instinctively have quit it: there they hoist us

To cry to the sea that roared to us...

Metaphors: Describing one thing as something else to express what it is like. The tiny, leaky boat is described as a "rotten carcass", an animal's dead body. The sea "roared to us" – making it sound like a creature speaking to them.

*
Assonance: Patterns of similar sounds that echo each other.

**
Alliteration: Pairs or patterns of words or syllables with the same first letter.

***
Repetition: Repeating similar words or phrases to reinforce an idea.

Everyday speech

Some parts of the play are not in blank verse, but in prose, like normal speech. Shakespeare often used this style for servants, and in *The Tempest* it's mainly Trinculo and Stephano who speak like this.

TRINCULO: Alas, the storm
is come again!
My best way is to creep
under his gaberdine*;
there is no other shelter
hereabout: misery acquaints
a man with strange
bedfellows!

*cloak

Did you know?

Many modern words and phrases first appeared in Shakespeare's works, and he may even have invented some of them. In *The Tempest*, they include:

Leaky   Watchdog   Eyeball
In a pickle   Sea change

WHAT *THE TEMPEST* MEANS NOW

The Tempest is still popular today, even though it's over 400 years since Shakespeare wrote it, and the English language has changed a huge amount in that time. Besides being performed as a play, it's inspired many paintings, and been turned into operas, ballets, films, puppet shows, and a musical, *Return to the Forbidden Planet*.

For all time

This is partly because Shakespeare was so good at putting together a story and making it work well on stage. It's also because *The Tempest*, like his other plays, focuses on themes and topics that are interesting and relevant to everyone throughout history, not just his own audiences. As his friend Ben Jonson said...

He was not of an age, but for all time.

Getting older

As Shakespeare reached the end of his career, he wrote comedies that feature not just young lovers, but their parents too. The romances explore what it's like for parents when their children grow up, and how young people relate to an older, more traditional generation. Whenever you live in history, that's something that never changes!

Lost and found

The story of losing something, searching for it and finally finding it again has been around since ancient times. You'll see it in children's books, films, novels and computer games. It's a simple but powerful plot that everyone can relate to – so we feel deeply for Alonso and Ferdinand when they both think the other is drowned, then when they are reunited. The King's ship, Prospero's dukedom, and Ariel's freedom are also lost and found in the play.

The Island

The Tempest is set on an island, which is another eternally popular theme. There are books, poems and films from all eras that explore the idea of a self-contained island and the mini-society that can develop there.

William Golding's famous novel *Lord of the Flies* explored what might happen if a group of schoolboys were left to survive on a deserted island.

TV series *Lost* was set on a mysterious island where a group of strangers had survived a plane crash.

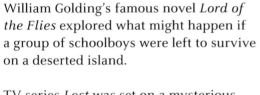

The island
on *Lost*

*Lord of the
Flies*

WHAT SHAKESPEARE DID NEXT

If *The Tempest* really was Shakespeare's farewell
to writing plays, what did he do afterwards?

Shakespeare's family

While Shakespeare spent a large part of his life working in
London, his family stayed in his home town, Stratford-upon-
Avon, 160km (100 miles) away. He had a wife, Anne, who he had
married when he was only 18, and three children, Susanna, the
oldest, and Judith and Hamnet, who were twins. Sadly, Hamnet
died in 1596, aged 11.

Shakespeare often visited Stratford and in 1597, he had earned
enough money from his career to buy a big, grand house there,
called New Place, for his family to live in.

Going home

Shakespeare finally retired and moved back to Stratford to live
at New Place, probably in 1610 – around the same time that he
wrote *The Tempest*. He still went on trips to London, and had
many friends in the city, but he no longer lived there.

Last works

The Tempest was not actually Shakespeare's last play – he went on to write three more. But these last works were collaborations, written with another well known playwright, John Fletcher. They are *The Two Noble Kinsmen*, *Henry VIII*, and *Cardenio*.

Lost play

Though records show the Kings' Men performed *Cardenio* in 1613, this play was lost long ago and no one knows what was in it. But maybe there's a still a copy out there, somewhere!

Shakespeare's death

After just a few years living back in Stratford, Shakespeare died, on 23 April 1616, thought to be his 52nd birthday. He is buried in Stratford's Holy Trinity Church, with an epitaph warning that his grave and body must never be moved:

Good friend for Jesus sake forbeare,
To dig the dust enclosed here.
Blessed be the man that spares these stones,
And cursed be he that moves my bones.

GLOSSARY

alliteration	Grouping together words with the same initial letter
assonance	Grouping together words that sound similar
blank verse	Type of non-rhyming poetry used by Shakespeare
boatswain	Foreman of a ship's crew
cherubim	A little angel
dramatis personae	List of characters in a play
fathom	A measure of depth, roughly 1.8 m (6 feet)
jester	Clown or fool
melancholy	Sad or brooding
metaphor	Describing something as another thing to compare them
playwright	Author of plays
prose	Text written in ordinary sentences, not in verse
retinue	A group of assistants and followers
sea shanty	Traditional folk song sung by sailors
stage directions	Instructions for the actors in a play
supernatural	Magical or beyond the laws of nature
superstitious	Fear or belief about luck, magic or the supernatural
symbol	Something that stands for an idea or object

GLOSSARY OF SHAKESPEARE'S LANGUAGE

abjure	give up
afeard	afraid
art	are
bark	boat
bestir	move yourself
cell	hut or small cottage
didst	did
doth	does
gaberdine	cloak
hath	has
quaint	clever or ingenious
rapt	absorbed, entranced
thee	you
thou	you
yarely	quickly

THE TEMPEST QUIZ

Test yourself and your friends on
the story, characters and language
of Shakespeare's *The Tempest*. You can find
the answers at the bottom of the page.

1) Who tells King Alonso and his friends to go back
   below deck?
2) Which kingdom does King Alonso rule over?
3) What did Gonzalo do to save Prospero and Miranda?
4) Who is Sycorax's son?
5) In Ariel's song, what do King Alonso's eyes turn into?
6) What does Miranda's name mean?
7) What excuse do Antonio and Sebastian make up for
   drawing their daggers?
8) Where does Stephano get stuck?
9) What does Prospero draw on the ground?
10) What are Ferdinand and Miranda doing when Alonso
    finds them?

10) Playing chess
9) A circle
8) In a slimy pond
7) They heard the roaring of lions
6) Admired
5) Pearls
4) Caliban
3) Packed their boat with food, water and belongings
2) Naples.
1) The boatswain

MACBETH
978 0 7502 9109 5

HAMLET
978 0 7502 9113 2

A MIDSUMMER NIGHT'S DREAM
978 0 7502 9110 1

THE TEMPEST
978 0 7502 9115 6

ROMEO AND JULIET
978 0 7502 9111 8

MUCH ADO ABOUT NOTHING
978 0 7502 9114 9

SAINT BENEDICT CATHOLIC
VOLUNTARY ACADEMY
DUFFIELD ROAD
DERBY
DE22 1JD